CAROLINA PANTHERS

BRENDAN FLYNN

WWW.APEXEDITIONS.COM

Copyright © 2025 by Apex Editions, Mendota Heights, MN 55120. All rights reserved. No part of this book may be reproduced or utilized in any form or by any means without written permission from the publisher.

Apex is distributed by North Star Editions:
sales@northstareditions.com | 888-417-0195

Produced for Apex by Red Line Editorial.

Photographs ©: Brian Westerholt/AP Images, cover, 1, 4–5, 58–59; Eakin Howard/Getty Images Sport/Getty Images, 6–7; Bob Leverone/The Charlotte Observer/AP Images, 8–9; Andy Lyons/Allsport/Getty Images Sport/Getty Images, 10–11; Craig Jones/Getty Images Sport/Getty Images, 12–13; Doug Benc/Getty Images Sport/Getty Images, 14–15; Ezra Shaw/Getty Images Sport/Getty Images, 16–17; Paul Spinelli/AP Images, 19, 57; Jamie Squire/Getty Images Sport/Getty Images, 20–21; Brian Bahr/Getty Images Sport/Getty Images, 22–23; Stephen Dunn/Getty Images Sport/Getty Images, 24–25; Bob Leverone/AP Images, 26–27, 32–33; Grant Halverson/Getty Images Sport/Getty Images, 28–29, 38–39; Michael Zagaris/Getty Images Sport/Getty Images, 30–31; Jared C. Tilton/Getty Images Sport/Getty Images, 34–35; Ronald Martinez/Getty Images Sport/Getty Images, 37; Shutterstock Images, 40–41, 42–43, 44–45, 50–51; Kevin Hoffman/Getty Images Sport/Getty Images, 47; Mark Elias/AP Images, 48–49; David Stluka/AP Images, 52–53; Scott Cunningham/Getty Images Sport/Getty Images, 54–55

Library of Congress Control Number: 2023921991

ISBN
979-8-89250-149-1 (hardcover)
979-8-89250-166-8 (paperback)
979-8-89250-290-0 (ebook pdf)
979-8-89250-183-5 (hosted ebook)

Printed in the United States of America
Mankato, MN
012025

NOTE TO PARENTS AND EDUCATORS

Apex books are designed to build literacy skills in striving readers. Exciting, high-interest content attracts and holds readers' attention. The text is carefully leveled to allow students to achieve success quickly.

TABLE OF CONTENTS

CHAPTER 1
KEEP POUNDING 4

CHAPTER 2
EARLY HISTORY 8

PLAYER SPOTLIGHT
JULIUS PEPPERS 18

CHAPTER 3
LEGENDS 20

CHAPTER 4
RECENT HISTORY 28

PLAYER SPOTLIGHT
STEVE SMITH 36

CHAPTER 5
MODERN STARS 38

PLAYER SPOTLIGHT
CAM NEWTON 46

CHAPTER 6
TEAM TRIVIA 48

TEAM RECORDS • 56
TIMELINE • 58
COMPREHENSION QUESTIONS • 60
GLOSSARY • 62
TO LEARN MORE • 63
ABOUT THE AUTHOR • 63
INDEX • 64

CHAPTER 1

KEEP POUNDING

The Carolina Panthers offense takes the field. It's the fourth quarter. The Panthers trail by one point. They have the ball on their own 9-yard line. Quarterback Bryce Young knows his team has a long way to go. But he doesn't panic.

The Panthers' stadium holds more than 74,000 fans.

Young takes his team past the 50-yard line. But soon, it's fourth down. Young stays calm. He completes a pass. Carolina is still alive. Then, Young leads his team inside the 20-yard line. Only three seconds remain. The Panthers kick an easy field goal. Carolina wins the game!

BANG THE DRUM

Before every Panthers home game, a huge drum is rolled onto the field. The drum reads "Keep Pounding." Every game, someone gets to bang the drum. Often, it's a famous person. Sometimes, it's a former player.

Bryce Young looks for a receiver during a 2023 game.

CHAPTER 2
EARLY HISTORY

The Carolina Panthers played their first game in 1995. They were an expansion team. Carolina entered the league the same year as the Jacksonville Jaguars. Head coach Dom Capers got the Panthers off to a solid start. He led the team to seven wins in 1995.

The Panthers' first-ever game was against the Atlanta Falcons.

Running back Anthony Johnson (23) pounds his way through the defense during Carolina's first playoff game.

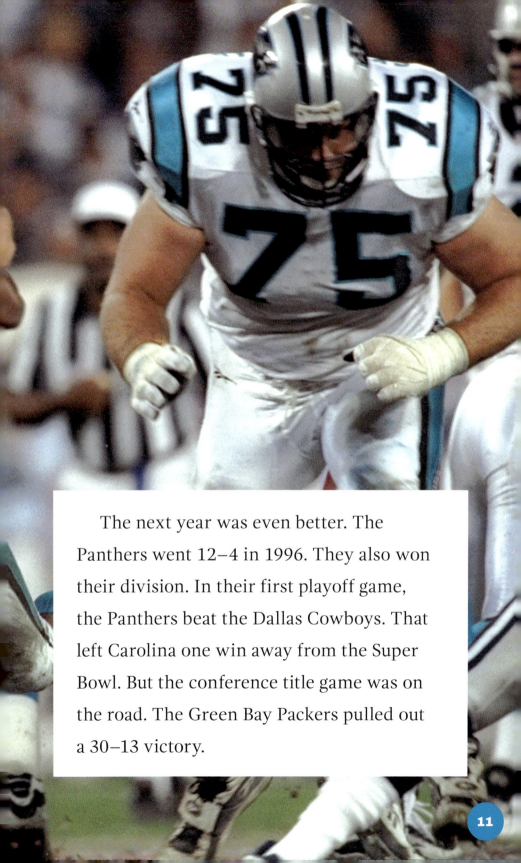

The next year was even better. The Panthers went 12–4 in 1996. They also won their division. In their first playoff game, the Panthers beat the Dallas Cowboys. That left Carolina one win away from the Super Bowl. But the conference title game was on the road. The Green Bay Packers pulled out a 30–13 victory.

The Panthers soon fell on hard times. They missed the playoffs the next six years. Carolina hit rock bottom in 2001. That season, the team posted a 1–15 record. The next year, a new head coach took over. John Fox guided the Panthers to seven wins in 2002.

STRONG START

Panthers rookie Steve Smith got the team off to a great start in 2001. In the first game of the season, he returned the opening kickoff for a touchdown. The Panthers went on to beat the Minnesota Vikings. But they lost the rest of their games that season.

Running back Lamar Smith (26) escapes from a defender during a win over the Detroit Lions in 2002.

In 2003, Carolina took another huge step forward. The Panthers went 11–5. Then they made it all the way to the Super Bowl. Carolina fought hard against the New England Patriots. The game was close. It came down to the final seconds. But the Patriots kicked a late field goal. Carolina lost 32–29.

PLAYOFF THRILLER

The Panthers faced the St. Louis Rams in the 2003 playoffs. The Panthers were up by 11 points. However, the Rams came back. They tied the game on the last play of the fourth quarter. Neither team scored in the first overtime period. Then, on the first play of the second overtime, Carolina scored the winning touchdown. Many Panthers fans call it the greatest game in team history.

Steve Smith scores the winning touchdown in a playoff game against the St. Louis Rams.

In the 2005 season, the Panthers made it back to the conference title game. They came up short, though. The Seattle Seahawks won 34–14.

Carolina won another division title in 2008. But they lost in the first round of the playoffs.

In 2010, the Panthers dropped to 2–14. The team fired head coach John Fox. Fans were frustrated with the team. But better days were just around the corner.

In the 2005 season, Carolina crushed the New York Giants 23–0 in the first round of the playoffs.

PLAYER SPOTLIGHT

JULIUS PEPPERS

Defensive end Julius Peppers grew up in North Carolina. Next, he played college football at the University of North Carolina. Then the Carolina Panthers selected him in the 2002 draft. He became the team's first homegrown star.

Peppers burst into the NFL. He had 12 sacks in his first season. He also won the Defensive Rookie of the Year Award. Peppers didn't stop there. He spent 10 seasons with the Panthers. In that time, he recorded 97 sacks.

JULIUS PEPPERS ENTERED THE PRO FOOTBALL HALL OF FAME IN 2024.

CHAPTER 3

LEGENDS

Quarterback Kerry Collins was Carolina's first-ever draft choice. He started for three seasons. He also led the Panthers to their first playoff win. Veteran quarterback Steve Beuerlein took over in 1998. The next season, he led the NFL in passing yards.

Kerry Collins tossed 47 touchdown passes during his time with the Panthers.

Muhsin Muhammad scores a touchdown against the Patriots during the Super Bowl.

The Panthers were stacked with talent in the early 2000s. Running back Stephen Davis rushed for 1,444 yards in 2003. And quarterback Jake Delhomme had plenty of great targets. In 2004, Muhsin Muhammad led the NFL in receiving yards and touchdown catches. The next year, Steve Smith led the league in catches, receiving yards, and touchdown catches.

EARLY STAR

Tight end Wesley Walls was one of Carolina's first stars. He joined the team in 1996. Walls was named to the Pro Bowl in five of the next six years. His best year came in 1999. Walls recorded 63 catches for 822 yards. He also scored 12 touchdowns.

Julius Peppers was one of the NFL's top defensive ends of the 2000s. He spent several seasons playing with Kris Jenkins. Jenkins was a massive defensive tackle. He was great at stuffing runs. Jenkins earned three trips to the Pro Bowl in seven years.

SACK MASTER
Kevin Greene played just three of his 15 NFL seasons with the Panthers. His first year with the team came in 1996. That year, Greene led the NFL with 14.5 sacks. He added 27 more sacks in his last two seasons. Greene was a huge part of Carolina's early success.

Kris Jenkins (77) recorded 216 tackles during his years with the Panthers.

Veteran linebacker Sam Mills joined the Panthers in their first season. He soon became a team leader. In a 1996 game, Mills returned an interception for a touchdown. That play led the Panthers to their first-ever victory.

Linebacker Jon Beason was Carolina's top draft pick in 2007. He led the team in tackles in each of his first three seasons.

INTERCEPTION EXPERTS

Safety Mike Minter was a key part of the Panthers' secondary. In 2003, he returned two interceptions for scores. Cornerback Chris Gamble arrived the next year. Gamble picked off 13 passes in his first two seasons.

Chris Gamble returns an interception during a 2011 game against the Tennessee Titans.

CHAPTER 4

RECENT HISTORY

The Panthers hired Ron Rivera as head coach in 2011. It was Rivera's first head coaching job. But he quickly turned the team around. Rivera led Carolina to division titles in 2013 and 2014.

Ron Rivera salutes the fans after a win in the 2014 season.

Running back Jonathan Stewart scores a diving touchdown during the Super Bowl.

In 2015, Rivera and quarterback Cam Newton led the Panthers to a 15–1 record. Then the team notched two playoff wins. Carolina was back in the Super Bowl. The Panthers kept the game close. They trailed by just six points in the fourth quarter. But the Denver Broncos pulled away. Carolina lost 24–10.

STREAKING

The Panthers won their final four games of the 2014 regular season. Then they started the next season 14–0. It was an 18-game regular-season winning streak. That was the third-longest in NFL history.

Quarterback Cam Newton dances into the end zone during a 2017 game against the Philadelphia Eagles.

The year after their Super Bowl run, the Panthers stumbled. They finished the 2016 season with a losing record. They bounced back in 2017. That year, they went 11–5. But they lost in the first round of the playoffs. After that, the team went downhill. Rivera was fired in 2019.

NEW FACES

The Panthers had six head coaches between 2019 and 2023. Matt Ruhle lasted the longest. His teams won five games in 2020 and 2021. But Ruhle was fired after a 1–4 start in 2022. Dave Canales took over in 2024.

In 2023, the Panthers needed a quarterback. To get one, the team made a bold move. The Chicago Bears had the first pick in the draft. So, Carolina traded four draft picks and one player to Chicago. In return, Carolina got the top pick. They used it to select quarterback Bryce Young. Young led the Panthers to just two wins in 2023. But he gained lots of experience. Fans hoped he would soon become a star.

Bryce Young topped 2,800 passing yards in his rookie season.

PLAYER SPOTLIGHT

STEVE SMITH

Wide receiver Steve Smith was a third-round pick in the 2001 draft. It didn't take long for him to become a playmaker. In his first game, he returned the opening kickoff for a touchdown.

Smith was smaller than most receivers. But he was strong and fast. In the 2003 playoffs, Smith scored a 69-yard touchdown. That play helped Carolina beat the Rams. In 2005, Smith had his best season ever. He led the NFL in catches, receiving yards, and touchdowns.

STEVE SMITH SCORED 75 TOUCHDOWNS DURING HIS 13 YEARS WITH THE PANTHERS.

CHAPTER 5

MODERN STARS

Quarterback Cam Newton led the Panthers from 2011 to 2019. Newton became one of the league's biggest stars. His favorite target was tight end Greg Olsen. Olsen posted three straight 1,000-yard seasons. He was the first tight end in NFL history to do that.

Greg Olsen scored 39 touchdowns during his nine years with Carolina.

In 2008, DeAngelo Williams led the NFL with 20 touchdowns.

DeAngelo Williams and Jonathan Stewart played together in Carolina from 2008 to 2014. The running back duo was known as "Double Trouble." They made history in 2009. Both players ran for more than 1,100 yards. They were the first teammates to do that in the same year.

BIG BLOCKER

"Double Trouble" got a big assist from the team's offensive line. Ryan Kalil led the way. Kalil was a five-time Pro Bowl pick. He earned the Panthers' starting center job in 2008. Kalil spent 12 seasons with the Panthers. He started 145 games.

Linebacker Luke Kuechly made a splash in 2012. He finished the season as the NFL's leading tackler. He also won the Defensive Rookie of the Year Award. The next season, he was named the Defensive Player of the Year.

Kuechly had plenty of help on defense. Linebacker Thomas Davis spent 13 seasons with Carolina. He recorded more than 1,000 tackles.

Luke Kuechly (59) recorded 1,092 tackles during his career.

Christian McCaffrey piled up 2,392 total yards in 2019.

Running back Christian McCaffrey started his career with the Panthers. In 2019, he led the NFL in total yards. From 2019 to 2021, wide receiver D. J. Moore posted three straight 1,000-yard seasons. The Panthers traded McCaffrey in 2022. And they traded Moore in 2023. The Moore trade helped Carolina land quarterback Bryce Young.

D-LINE STAR

The 2023 Panthers built their defensive line around Derrick Brown. The massive defensive tackle made a career-high 103 tackles that year. He also earned his first Pro Bowl nod.

PLAYER SPOTLIGHT

CAM NEWTON

Quarterback Cam Newton was the first pick of the 2011 draft. And he lived up to the hype. Newton threw for 422 yards in his first game. The next week, he threw for 432 yards.

Newton was a threat on the ground, too. He ended his rookie year with 14 rushing touchdowns. At the time, that was the most ever by a quarterback.

In 2015, Newton led the Panthers to the Super Bowl. He was also named the league's Most Valuable Player (MVP).

CAM NEWTON THREW FOR MORE THAN 29,000 YARDS DURING HIS 10 YEARS WITH CAROLINA.

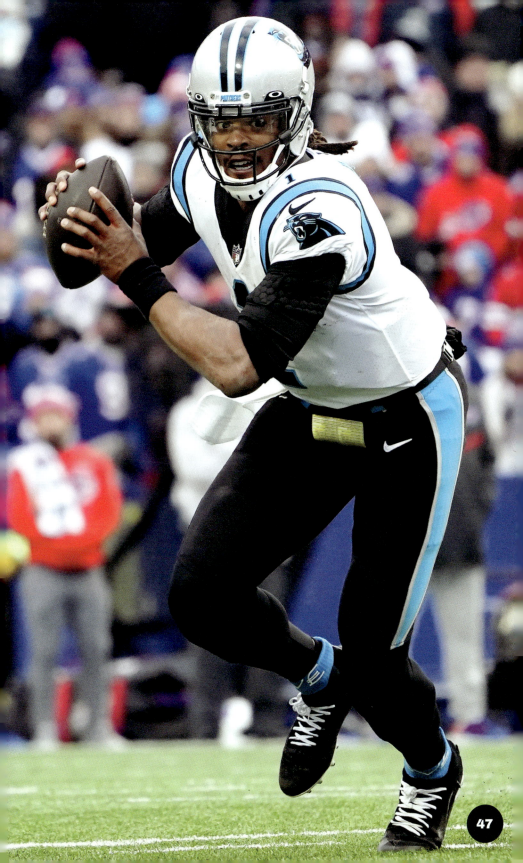

CHAPTER 6
TEAM TRIVIA

In 1993, the NFL announced that Carolina would get a team. Team owner Jerry Richardson had to come up with a name. His son Mark suggested the Panthers. Mark said panthers are "powerful, sleek, and strong." He said those are all things the team should be.

Panthers owner Jerry Richardson shows off the team's helmet in 1993.

The Panthers' stadium is also home to Charlotte FC of Major League Soccer.

North Carolina and South Carolina are both football hotbeds. The Panthers wanted to draw fans from both states. So, the team didn't use North or South in its name. The Panthers have even played home games in both states. They played their first season in Clemson, South Carolina. Their new stadium opened the next year. It's in Charlotte, North Carolina.

SHOWING SUPPORT

It took a while to convince the NFL that the Carolinas could support an NFL team. From 1989 to 1991, three preseason games took place in the area. Two were in North Carolina. One was in South Carolina. All three games sold out.

The Tampa Bay Buccaneers are one of the Panthers' biggest rivals.

The Carolinas are on the East Coast. But the NFC East already had five teams when the Panthers joined the league. The NFC West had only four teams. So, the Panthers were added to that division. It made for lots of long road trips. The league created new divisions in 2002. Carolina joined the NFC South.

FIRST RIVALRY

The Panthers quickly built a rivalry with the San Francisco 49ers. The two teams were more than 2,700 miles (4,300 km) apart. But they battled for control of the NFC West for several years.

53

Sam Mills was voted into the Pro Football Hall of Fame in 2022.

Sam Mills became Carolina's linebackers coach after he stopped playing. Before the 2003 season, he found out he had cancer. Doctors said he had just three months to live. Mills refused to give up. He gave a speech to the team. He said, "I'm a fighter. I kept pounding. You're fighters too. Keep pounding!" Mills lived for more than a year and a half. And "Keep Pounding" has been the team's rallying cry ever since.

TEAM RECORDS

All-Time Passing Yards: 29,725
  Cam Newton (2011–19, 2021)

All-Time Touchdown Passes: 186
  Cam Newton (2011–19, 2021)

All-Time Rushing Yards: 7,318
  Jonathan Stewart (2008–17)

All-Time Receiving Yards: 12,197
  Steve Smith (2001–13)

All-Time Touchdowns: 75
  Steve Smith (2001–13)

All-Time Interceptions: 27
  Chris Gamble (2004–12)

All-Time Sacks: 97
  Julius Peppers (2002–09, 2017–18)

All-Time Scoring: 1,482
  John Kasay (1995–2010)

All-Time Games Played: 243
  J. J. Jansen (2009–)

All-Time Coaching Wins: 76
  Ron Rivera (2011–19)

All statistics are accurate through 2023.

TIMELINE

1995 — The Carolina Panthers play their first season and win seven games.

1996 — In their second season, the Panthers reach the conference title game.

2003 — The Panthers go 11–5 and reach their first Super Bowl. They lose to the New England Patriots on a late field goal.

2005 — The Panthers reach the conference title game again but fall to the Seattle Seahawks.

2011 — Ron Rivera takes over as head coach and makes Cam Newton the team's top draft pick.

2013 — The Panthers go 12–4 and win the first of three straight NFC South titles.

2015 — Newton wins the MVP Award and leads the Panthers to the Super Bowl, but they lose to the Denver Broncos.

2019 — Running back Christian McCaffrey ends the season with 1,387 rushing yards and 1,005 receiving yards, making him the third player in NFL history to top 1,000 yards in both categories.

2022 — Former Panthers linebacker and coach Sam Mills is voted into the Pro Football Hall of Fame 17 years after his death from cancer.

2023 — The Panthers trade for the No. 1 pick in the draft and select quarterback Bryce Young.

COMPREHENSION QUESTIONS

Write your answers on a separate piece of paper.

1. Write a paragraph that explains the main ideas of Chapter 2.

2. Who do you think was the greatest player in Panthers history? Why?

3. Who passed for more than 400 yards in each of his first two NFL games?
   - A. Bryce Young
   - B. Kerry Collins
   - C. Cam Newton

4. Why was it a surprise that the Panthers reached the conference title game in 1996?
   - A. Expansion teams usually take a long time to become good.
   - B. No team from the NFC West had ever made it that far.
   - C. The Panthers had a rookie quarterback that season.

5. What does **stumbled** mean in this book?

*The year after their Super Bowl run, the Panthers **stumbled**. They finished the 2016 season with a losing record.*

    A. played well
    B. played poorly
    C. moved to a new city

6. What does **draw** mean in this book?

*The Panthers wanted to **draw** fans from both states. So, the team didn't use North or South in its name.*

    A. to make a picture
    B. to bring in
    C. to win a game

Answer key on page 64.

GLOSSARY

conference
A group of teams that make up part of a sports league.

division
In the NFL, a group of teams that make up part of a conference.

expansion team
A new team that is added to a league.

interception
A pass that is caught by a defensive player.

overtime
An extra period that happens if two teams are tied at the end of the fourth quarter.

playoffs
A set of games played after the regular season to decide which team is the champion.

rivalry
An ongoing competition that brings out strong emotion from fans and players.

sacks
Plays that happen when a defender tackles the quarterback before he can throw the ball.

secondary
The defensive players, such as cornerbacks and safeties, who start the play farthest from the line of scrimmage.

veteran
A person who has been doing his or her job for a long time and has a lot of experience.

TO LEARN MORE

BOOKS

Coleman, Ted. *Carolina Panthers All-Time Greats*. Mendota Heights, MN: Press Box Books, 2022.

Goldstein, Margaret J. *Meet Bryce Young: Carolina Panthers Superstar*. Minneapolis: Lerner Publications, 2025.

Whiting, Jim. *The Story of the Carolina Panthers*. Mankato, MN: Creative Education, 2025.

ONLINE RESOURCES

Visit **www.apexeditions.com** to find links and resources related to this title.

ABOUT THE AUTHOR

Brendan Flynn is a San Francisco resident and an author of numerous children's books. In addition to writing about sports, Flynn also enjoys competing in triathlons, Scrabble tournaments, and chili cook-offs.

INDEX

Beason, Jon, 26
Beuerlein, Steve, 20
Brown, Derrick, 45

Capers, Dom, 8
Collins, Kerry, 20

Davis, Stephen, 23
Davis, Thomas, 42
Delhomme, Jake, 23

Fox, John, 12, 16

Gamble, Chris, 26
Greene, Kevin, 24

Jenkins, Kris, 24

Kalil, Ryan, 41
Kuechly, Luke, 42

McCaffrey, Christian, 45

Mills, Sam, 26, 55
Minter, Mike, 26
Moore, D. J., 45
Muhammad, Muhsin, 23

Newton, Cam, 31, 38, 46

Olsen, Greg, 38

Peppers, Julius, 18, 24

Rivera, Ron, 28, 31, 33

Smith, Steve, 12, 23, 36
Stewart, Jonathan, 41

Walls, Wesley, 23
Williams, DeAngelo, 41

Young, Bryce, 5, 6, 35, 45

ANSWER KEY:
1. Answers will vary; 2. Answers will vary; 3. C; 4. A; 5. B; 6. B